GRATITUDE

JOURNAL

A DAILY APPRECIATION

THIS JOURNAL BELONGS TO

_____

ISBN-13: 978-1514818022

ISBN-10: 1514818027

Limits of Liability and Disclaimer of Warranty

The author and publisher shall not be liable for your misuse of this material. This book is strictly for informational and educational purposes.

Gratitude

Gratitude is appreciation for every moment in your life. It is a feeling of abundance. It is saying thank you to the Universe for what you have right now.

Write down two to five things you are grateful for every day, and you will see your life slowly transform. Make this your daily ritual. Instead of focusing on what you don't have, this process makes you find a way to be grateful for what you do have.

First, every gratitude journal entry needs to be positive and written in the present tense:

I am grateful for the health and well-being of my family.

Second, if a challenging thing has happened that day, write down what you have learned from this experience:

I am grateful that my friend and I are mending our differences. I am learning to trust in the wisdom of life.

Third, try to be specific:

I am grateful to have found an exercise partner.

Gratitude makes you happier and more optimistic, improving your health and relationships and boosting your overall well-being.

Your gratitude should be directed towards everything that you are creating in this life. It is the foundation of your life and is integral to all your experiences. It is a state of mind that you need to feel before your desires can manifest into your reality.

You need to start feeling gratitude as you set your intentions. Intentions are the starting point for fulfilling your dreams. Intentions can be powerful if they are combined with gratitude, as they tell the Universe exactly what you want right now. Intentions are a process by which we exercise our true powers as humans: intentions manifest only when we are living our life in gratitude and appreciation and stop expecting an outcome. Hence, surrendering to the now in appreciation is a way for our dreams to manifest. Let go of your desires; live every minute doing things you enjoy, and trust that what you desire will happen – then it will appear in your life.

As soon as you have set your intentions and filled your life with gratitude, your desires come true. You just need to have patience, gratitude, and absolute faith that what you desire will come. The Universe also needs to be absolutely certain that this is what you really want. If you want something, you might see it everywhere you go. Acknowledge that the Universe is testing you to see whether this is what you really want. Feel joy and excitement when you see what you desire.

Experiencing wonder is better than wishing. Wishing keeps you in a state of expectation, while appreciating the wonders in your life can help you feel excitement about what you already have. It makes you feel that everything and anything is possible.

Gratitude is also an important component to align your goals with your subconscious mind.

How can you align yourself with your subconscious? Three things are important: (1) Have a clear mind. It is important to be clear about what you want. This is why there is always a time delay before we get what we want. As time goes by, you become clearer about what you really want. (2) Focus: it is important to focus on your desires. Energy flows where focus goes. Focus your energy and action on your desire. (3) Be grateful. Always be grateful for what you have. If you cannot find one thing to be grateful for, then be grateful for the biggest gift in your life – your breath.

It is sometimes easier to align with our deeper self when we are facing challenges. This is because, when we get rid of ego and look beyond our bodies, we can feel our alignment to our higher self and our source. Challenges are our biggest teachers. Nothing teaches us more in life than challenges. They are the fastest way to find our authentic self. Our egoless spirit aligns with the Universe. Therefore, it is important to be truthful in your gratitude journal. Write down what you learned from your challenges.

Giving is a good way to align yourself with the Universe as well. We always feel better when we give to others. When we give to others and expect something in return, then we will only be disappointed. When we give, we are giving to the Universe, our source. We already have so much to be grateful for. Recording your giving in your journal can show how full your life is as well.

There is also power in receiving help. To receive help is to remove our ego. We can be in alignment when we receive from others. The important thing to remember is to be grateful and not feel entitled.

We must strive to live with purpose. When we live with purpose, we feel good inside.

You will note a pattern emerging after a few days of

recording things you are grateful for. You will notice miracles. Miracles can be big or small. There are miracles every day. A miracle is something that happens that is extremely improbable. What do you do when you encounter a miracle? (1) Recognize the miracle. (2) Appreciate it. (3) Say thank you to the Universe. Also, always record these miracles in your gratitude journal. More miracles will come into your life when you are appreciative. Gratitude is giving thanks for this moment that the Universe has created for you. Start now and write two to five things every day that you are grateful for, and watch your life transform.

Transformations

Use this section to keep a monthly log of transformations in your life. Your transformations may be physical, mental, or spiritual. You may have found joy in your life, you may feel more relaxed, there may be improvements in your health, you may be sleeping better, you may feel more connected with people, or you may have increased energy. Write about all your transformations. As you continue with your daily ritual of recording things, you can acknowledge transformations in your life. You don't need to wait until the end of the month to record transformations. Do it regularly. When you review past entries from your daily gratitude journal and this monthly transformations log, you will see a pattern to your life's journey. You will also notice where your life is focused. Energy flows where focus goes. What percentage of your focus is going into your work, children, relationship, health, and finances? What percentage of your focus is going into your growth and development? You will find that you attract more of what you are grateful for. Positive thoughts attract positive things from the Universe. Keeping a log of transformations will show you how far you have come in your journey.

Gratitude

Never lose an opportunity of seeing anything
beautiful, for beauty is God's handwriting.

-Ralph Waldo Emerson

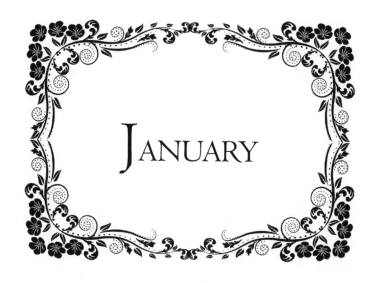

JANUARY

Gratitude is the inward feeling of kindness received. Thankfulness is the natural impulse to express that feeling. Thanksgiving is the following of that impulse.

-Henry Van Dyke

If the only prayer you say in your life is thank you, that would suffice.

-Meister Eckhart

JANUARY 1

_____

_____

_____

_____

JANUARY 2

_____

_____

_____

_____

JANUARY 3

_____

_____

_____

_____

JANUARY 4

JANUARY 5

JANUARY 6

JANUARY 7

JANUARY 8

JANUARY 9

JANUARY 10

JANUARY 11

A single grateful thought toward heaven is the most perfect prayer.

-Gotthold Ephraim Lessing

JANUARY 12

JANUARY 13

JANUARY 14

There is only one thing that can form a bond between men, and that is gratitude... we cannot give someone else greater power over us than we have ourselves.

-Charles de Secondat

JANUARY 15

JANUARY 16

JANUARY 17

JANUARY 18

JANUARY 19

JANUARY 20

JANUARY 21

JANUARY 22

JANUARY 23

JANUARY 24

JANUARY 25

Gratitude is not only the greatest of virtues, but the parent of all the others.

-Marcus Tullius Cicero

JANUARY 26

_____

_____

_____

_____

JANUARY 27

_____

_____

_____

_____

JANUARY 28

_____

_____

_____

_____

The pleasure which we most rarely experience gives us greatest delight.

-Epictetus

JANUARY 29

JANUARY 30

JANUARY 31

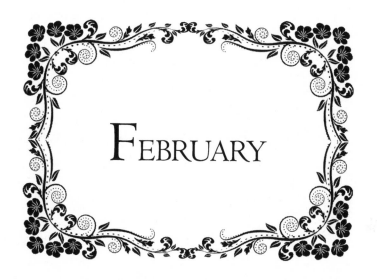

FEBRUARY

The happiness of life is made up of minute
fractions – the little, soon forgotten charities
of a kiss or a smile, a kind look or heartfelt
compliment, and the countless infinitesimals of
pleasurable and genial feeling.

-Samuel Taylor Coleridge

The essence of all beautiful art, all great art, is gratitude.

-Friedrich Nietzsche

FEBRUARY 1

_____

_____

_____

_____

_____

FEBRUARY 2

_____

_____

_____

_____

FEBRUARY 3

_____

_____

_____

_____

FEBRUARY 4

FEBRUARY 5

FEBRUARY 6

FEBRUARY 7

FEBRUARY 8

FEBRUARY 9

FEBRUARY 10

FEBRUARY 11

Saying thank you is more than good manners. It is good spirituality.

-Alfred Agache

FEBRUARY 12

FEBRUARY 13

FEBRUARY 14

Gratitude is the sign of noble souls.

-Aesop Fables

FEBRUARY 15

_____

_____

_____

_____

_____

FEBRUARY 16

_____

_____

_____

_____

_____

FEBRUARY 17

_____

_____

_____

_____

_____

FEBRUARY 18

FEBRUARY 19

FEBRUARY 20

FEBRUARY 21

FEBRUARY 22

FEBRUARY 23

FEBRUARY 24

FEBRUARY 25

Let us be grateful to people who make us happy, they are the charming gardeners who make our souls blossom.

-Marcel Proust

FEBRUARY 26

FEBRUARY 27

FEBRUARY 28

The beginning is the most important part of the work.

-Plato

FEBRUARY 29

_____

_____

_____

_____

_____

MARCH

No one is so completely disenchanted with the world, or knows it so thoroughly, or is so utterly disgusted with it, that when it begins to smile upon him he does not become partially reconciled to it.

-Giacomo Leopardi

The most wasted day of all is that on which we have not laughed.

-Nicolas Chamfort

MARCH 1

_____

_____

_____

_____

_____

MARCH 2

_____

_____

_____

_____

MARCH 3

_____

_____

_____

_____

MARCH 4

MARCH 5

MARCH 6

MARCH 7

MARCH 8

MARCH 9

MARCH 10

MARCH 11

Gratitude is a duty which ought to be paid, but which none have a right to expect.

-Jean-Jacques Rousseau

MARCH 12

MARCH 13

MARCH 14

Be content with what you have; rejoice in the way things are. When you realize there is nothing lacking, the whole world belongs to you.

-Lao Tzu

MARCH 15

MARCH 16

MARCH 17

MARCH 18

MARCH 19

MARCH 20

MARCH 21

MARCH 22

MARCH 23

MARCH 24

MARCH 25

Appreciation is a wonderful thing: It makes what is excellent in others belong to us as well.

-Voltaire

MARCH 26

MARCH 27

MARCH 28

You traverse the world in search of happiness, which is within the reach of every man. A contented mind confers it on all.

-Horace

MARCH 29

_____

_____

_____

_____

_____

MARCH 30

_____

_____

_____

_____

MARCH 31

_____

_____

_____

_____

APRIL

God has two dwellings; one in heaven, and the other in a meek and thankful heart.

-Izaak Walton

Prayer should be the key of the day and the lock of the night.

-George Herbert

APRIL 1

_____

_____

_____

_____

_____

APRIL 2

_____

_____

_____

_____

APRIL 3

_____

_____

_____

_____

APRIL 4

APRIL 5

APRIL 6

APRIL 7

APRIL 8

APRIL 9

APRIL 10

APRIL 11

The ultimate value of life depends upon awareness and the power of contemplation rather than upon mere survival.

-Aristotle

APRIL 12

APRIL 13

APRIL 14

Our greatest glory is not in never falling, but in rising every time we fall.

-Confucius

APRIL 15

APRIL 16

APRIL 17

APRIL 18

APRIL 19

APRIL 20

APRIL 21

APRIL 22

APRIL 23

APRIL 24

APRIL 25

For after all, the best thing one can do when it is raining is to let it rain.

-Henry Wadsworth Longfellow

APRIL 26

_____

_____

_____

_____

APRIL 27

_____

_____

_____

_____

APRIL 28

_____

_____

_____

_____

A daily practice of appreciation can transform one's life.

APRIL 29

_____

_____

_____

_____

_____

APRIL 30

_____

_____

_____

_____

_____

MAY

There exists only the present instant… a Now which always and without end is itself new. There is no yesterday nor any tomorrow, but only Now, as it was a thousand years ago and as it will be a thousand years since.

-Meister Eckhart

Life in abundance comes only through great love.

-Elbert Hubbard

MAY 1

_____

_____

_____

_____

_____

MAY 2

_____

_____

_____

_____

MAY 3

_____

_____

_____

_____

MAY 4

MAY 5

MAY 6

MAY 7

MAY 8

MAY 9

MAY 10

MAY 11

The trees that are slow to grow bear the best fruit.

-Moliere

MAY 12

MAY 13

MAY 14

To the generous mind the heaviest debt is that of gratitude, when it is not in our power to repay it.

-Benjamin Franklin

MAY 15

_____

MAY 16

_____

MAY 17

_____

MAY 18

MAY 19

MAY 20

MAY 21

MAY 22

MAY 23

MAY 24

MAY 25

The art of being happy lies in the power of extracting happiness from common things.

-Henry Ward Beecher

MAY 26

_____

_____

_____

_____

_____

MAY 27

_____

_____

_____

_____

_____

MAY 28

_____

_____

_____

_____

_____

Thou hast created me not from necessity but from grace.

-Solomon Ibn Gabirol

MAY 29

MAY 30

MAY 31

JUNE

For prayer is nothing else than being on terms of
friendship with God.

-Saint Teresa of Avila

Courtesies of a small and trivial character are the ones which strike deepest in the grateful and appreciating heart.

-Henry Clay

JUNE 1

JUNE 2

JUNE 3

JUNE 4

JUNE 5

JUNE 6

JUNE 7

JUNE 8

JUNE 9

JUNE 10

JUNE 11

Gratitude is a state of being and should be directed towards everything that you are creating in this life.

JUNE 12

_____

_____

_____

_____

JUNE 13

_____

_____

_____

_____

JUNE 14

_____

_____

_____

_____

When unhappy, one doubts everything; when happy, one doubts nothing.

-Joseph Roux

JUNE 15

_____

_____

_____

_____

_____

JUNE 16

_____

_____

_____

_____

JUNE 17

_____

_____

_____

_____

JUNE 18

JUNE 19

JUNE 20

JUNE 21

JUNE 22

_____

_____

_____

_____

_____

JUNE 23

_____

_____

_____

_____

_____

JUNE 24

_____

_____

_____

_____

JUNE 25

_____

_____

_____

_____

By doubting we are led to question, by questioning
we arrive at the truth.

-Peter Abelard

JUNE 26

JUNE 27

JUNE 28

We have it in our power to begin the world over again.

-Thomas Paine

JUNE 29

JUNE 30

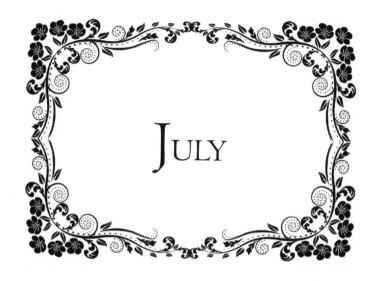

JULY

To the mind that is still, the whole universe surrenders.

-Lao Tzu

Learning never exhausts the mind.

-Leonardo da Vinci

JULY 1

_____

_____

_____

_____

_____

JULY 2

_____

_____

_____

_____

JULY 3

_____

_____

_____

_____

JULY 4

JULY 5

JULY 6

JULY 7

JULY 8

JULY 9

JULY 10

JULY 11

Showing up is the most important thing you can do for a friend.

JULY 12

_____

_____

_____

_____

JULY 13

_____

_____

_____

_____

JULY 14

_____

_____

_____

_____

To live is so startling it leaves little time for anything else.

-Emily Dickinson

JULY 15

_____

_____

_____

_____

_____

JULY 16

_____

_____

_____

_____

JULY 17

_____

_____

_____

_____

JULY 18

JULY 19

JULY 20

JULY 21

JULY 22

JULY 23

JULY 24

JULY 25

A loving heart is the beginning of all knowledge.

-Thomas Carlyle

JULY 26

JULY 27

JULY 28

Let us learn to appreciate there will be times when the trees will be bare, and look forward to the time when we may pick the fruit.

-Anton Chekhov

JULY 29

_____

_____

_____

_____

_____

JULY 30

_____

_____

_____

_____

JULY 31

_____

_____

_____

_____

AUGUST

True wisdom comes to each of us when we realize
how little we understand about life, ourselves, and
the world around us.

-Socrates

Our happiness depends on wisdom all the way.

-Sophocles

AUGUST 1

AUGUST 2

AUGUST 3

AUGUST 4

AUGUST 5

AUGUST 6

AUGUST 7

AUGUST 8

AUGUST 9

AUGUST 10

AUGUST 11

"I am" are the two most powerful words in your vocabulary. Use them wisely.

AUGUST 12

AUGUST 13

AUGUST 14

Love is the joy of the good, the wonder of the wise, the amazement of the Gods.

-Plato

AUGUST 15

AUGUST 16

AUGUST 17

AUGUST 18

AUGUST 19

AUGUST 20

AUGUST 21

AUGUST 22

AUGUST 23

AUGUST 24

AUGUST 25

Everyone has been made for some particular work, and the desire for that work has been put in every heart.

-Rumi

AUGUST 26

AUGUST 27

AUGUST 28

The most certain sign of wisdom is cheerfulness.

-Michel de Montaigne

AUGUST 29

AUGUST 30

AUGUST 31

SEPTEMBER

The great weight of the ship may indeed prevent
her from acquiring her greatest velocity; but when
she has attained it, she will advance by her own
intrinsic motion, without gaining any new degree
of velocity, or lessening what she has acquired.

-William Falconer

Habit, if not resisted, soon becomes necessity.

-Saint Augustine

SEPTEMBER 1

_____

_____

_____

_____

_____

SEPTEMBER 2

_____

_____

_____

_____

SEPTEMBER 3

_____

_____

_____

_____

SEPTEMBER 4

SEPTEMBER 5

SEPTEMBER 6

SEPTEMBER 7

SEPTEMBER 8

SEPTEMBER 9

SEPTEMBER 10

SEPTEMBER 11

Life consists not in holding good cards but in playing those you hold well.

-Josh Billings

SEPTEMBER 12

SEPTEMBER 13

SEPTEMBER 14

From a small seed a mighty trunk may grow.

-Aeschylus

SEPTEMBER 15

_____

_____

_____

_____

_____

SEPTEMBER 16

_____

_____

_____

_____

SEPTEMBER 17

_____

_____

_____

_____

SEPTEMBER 18

SEPTEMBER 19

SEPTEMBER 20

SEPTEMBER 21

SEPTEMBER 22

SEPTEMBER 23

SEPTEMBER 24

SEPTEMBER 25

Surround yourself with positive people who can raise you to a higher level.

SEPTEMBER 26

SEPTEMBER 27

SEPTEMBER 28

Happiness resides not in possessions, and not in gold, happiness dwells in the soul.

-Democritus

SEPTEMBER 29

SEPTEMBER 30

OCTOBER

He who postpones the hour of living is like the rustic who waits for the river to run out before he crosses.

-Horace

Events will take their course, it is no good of being angry at them; he is happiest who wisely turns them to the best account.

-Euripides

OCTOBER 1

_____

_____

_____

_____

_____

OCTOBER 2

_____

_____

_____

_____

OCTOBER 3

_____

_____

_____

_____

_____

OCTOBER 4

OCTOBER 5

OCTOBER 6

OCTOBER 7

OCTOBER 8

OCTOBER 9

OCTOBER 10

OCTOBER 11

Contentment consist not in adding more fuel, but in taking away some fire.

-Thomas Fuller

OCTOBER 12

OCTOBER 13

OCTOBER 14

A loving heart is the truest wisdom.

-Charles Dickens

OCTOBER 15

_____

_____

_____

_____

_____

OCTOBER 16

_____

_____

_____

_____

OCTOBER 17

_____

_____

_____

_____

OCTOBER 18

OCTOBER 19

OCTOBER 20

OCTOBER 21

OCTOBER 22

OCTOBER 23

OCTOBER 24

OCTOBER 25

Believe you can and you're halfway there.

-Theodore Roosevelt

OCTOBER 26

_____
_____
_____
_____
_____

OCTOBER 27

_____
_____
_____
_____
_____

OCTOBER 28

_____
_____
_____
_____
_____

A friend is one who knows you and loves you just the same.

-Elbert Hubbard

OCTOBER 29

OCTOBER 30

OCTOBER 31

NOVEMBER

For me the greatest beauty always lies in the greatest clarity.

-Gotthold Ephraim Lessing

Faith is to believe what you do not see; the reward of this faith is to see what you believe.

-Saint Augustine

NOVEMBER 1

_____

_____

_____

_____

NOVEMBER 2

_____

_____

_____

_____

NOVEMBER 3

_____

_____

_____

_____

NOVEMBER 4

NOVEMBER 5

NOVEMBER 6

NOVEMBER 7

NOVEMBER 8

NOVEMBER 9

NOVEMBER 10

NOVEMBER 11

There is no charm equal to tenderness of heart.

-Jane Austen

NOVEMBER 12

NOVEMBER 13

NOVEMBER 14

Confidence in the goodness of another is good proof of one's own goodness.

-Michel de Montaigne

NOVEMBER 15

NOVEMBER 16

NOVEMBER 17

NOVEMBER 18

NOVEMBER 19

NOVEMBER 20

NOVEMBER 21

NOVEMBER 22

NOVEMBER 23

NOVEMBER 24

NOVEMBER 25

There are more people who wish to be loved than there are who are willing to love.

-Nicolas Chamfort

NOVEMBER 26

_____

_____

_____

_____

_____

NOVEMBER 27

_____

_____

_____

_____

_____

NOVEMBER 28

_____

_____

_____

_____

_____

Men should strive to think much and know little.

-Democritus

NOVEMBER 29

_____
_____
_____
_____
_____

NOVEMBER 30

_____
_____
_____
_____
_____

December

As a single footstep will not make a path on the earth, so a single thought will not make a pathway in the mind. To make a deep physical path, we walk again and again. To make a deep mental path, we must think over and over the kind of thoughts we wish to dominate our lives.

-Henry David Thoreau

A tree is known by its fruit; a man by his deeds. A good deed is never lost; he who sows courtesy reaps friendship, and he who plants kindness gathers love.

-Saint Basil

DECEMBER 1

DECEMBER 2

DECEMBER 3

DECEMBER 4

DECEMBER 5

DECEMBER 6

DECEMBER 7

DECEMBER 8

DECEMBER 9

DECEMBER 10

DECEMBER 11

The best part of beauty is that which no picture can express.

-Francis Bacon

DECEMBER 12

DECEMBER 13

DECEMBER 14

Silence is the sleep that nourishes wisdom.

-Francis Bacon

DECEMBER 15

_____

_____

_____

_____

_____

DECEMBER 16

_____

_____

_____

_____

_____

DECEMBER 17

_____

_____

_____

_____

_____

DECEMBER 18

DECEMBER 19

DECEMBER 20

DECEMBER 21

DECEMBER 22

_____

DECEMBER 23

_____

DECEMBER 24

_____

DECEMBER 25

_____

All things must come to the soul from its roots, from where it is planted.

-Saint Teresa of Avila

DECEMBER 26

_____

_____

_____

_____

_____

DECEMBER 27

_____

_____

_____

_____

DECEMBER 28

_____

_____

_____

_____

Enthusiasm is the genius of sincerity; and truth accomplishes no victories without it.

-Edward G. Bulwer-Lytton

DECEMBER 29

DECEMBER 30

DECEMBER 31

TRANSFORMATIONS

To love oneself is the beginning of a lifelong
romance.

-Oscar Wilde

He who would learn to fly one day must first learn to stand and walk and run and climb and dance; one cannot fly into flying.

-Friedrich Nietzsche

JANUARY

Start by doing what's necessary; then do what's possible; and suddenly you are doing the impossible.

-Francis of Assisi

FEBRUARY

Miracles are not contrary to nature, but only contrary to what we know about nature.

-Saint Augustine

MARCH

_____

_____

_____

_____

_____

_____

_____

_____

_____

_____

_____

_____

_____

_____

_____

_____

_____

_____

_____

We know what we are, but know not what we may be.

-William Shakespeare

APRIL

Nothing can stop the man with the right mental attitude from achieving his goal; nothing on earth can help the man with the wrong mental attitude.

-Thomas Jefferson

MAY

Know what you want to do, hold the thought firmly, and do every day what should be done, and every sunset will see you that much nearer to your goal.

-Elbert Hubbard

JUNE

Where there is unity there is always victory.

-Publilius Syrus

JULY

Ask me not what I have, but what I am.

-Heinrich Heine

AUGUST

_____
_____
_____
_____
_____
_____
_____
_____
_____
_____
_____
_____
_____
_____
_____
_____
_____
_____

To be yourself in a world that is constantly trying to make you something else is the greatest achievement.

-Ralph Waldo Emerson

SEPTEMBER

It is never too late to be what you might have been.

-George Eliot

OCTOBER

What you think you are, you are, until you think otherwise.

-American Proverb

NOVEMBER

_____
_____
_____
_____
_____
_____
_____
_____
_____
_____
_____
_____
_____
_____
_____
_____
_____
_____
_____
_____
_____
_____

The journey of a thousand miles begins with one step.

-Lao Tzu

DECEMBER

THANK YOU

Made in the USA
Lexington, KY
09 November 2017